George

William R.

MARIA:

ANNA

George I

George R

William R.

Victoria R

Edward R & I

George R. I.

Edward R I

George R

Elizabeth R

W9-BSS-022

UNDOUBTED QUEEN

UNDOUBT

HUTCHINSON OF LONDON

ED QUEEN

COMPILED AND DESIGNED BY

H. TATLOCK MILLER

LOUDON SAINTHILL

CONTENTS

YOUR UNDOUBTED QUEEN

'SIRS

I HERE PRESENT UNTO YOU

QUEEN ELIZABETH

YOUR UNDOUBTED QUEEN

WHEREFORE

ALL YOU WHO ARE COME

THIS DAY TO DO YOUR

HOMAGE AND SERVICE

ARE YOU WILLING TO DO

THE SAME?'

From the Order of Coronation

HONI SOIT QVI MAL Y PENSE

DIEV ET MON DROIT

FANFARE FOR ELIZABETH

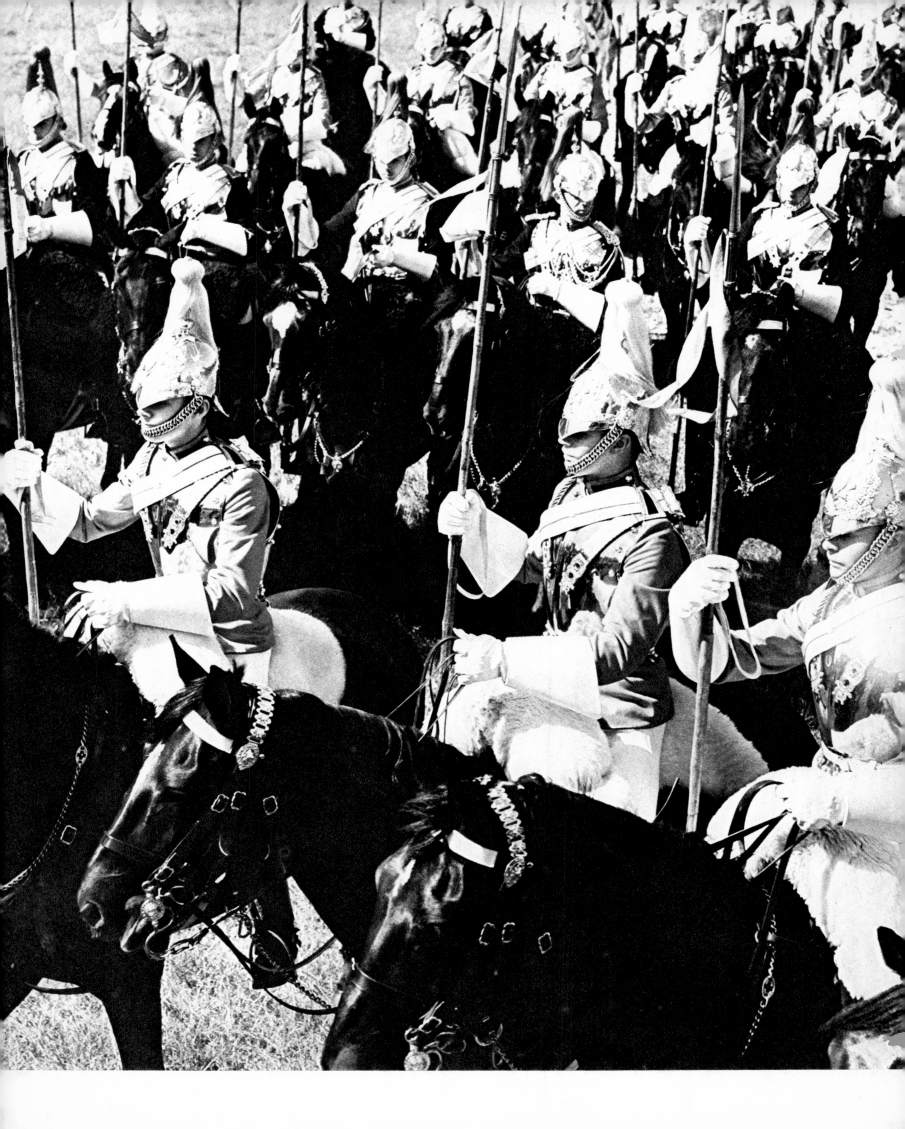

22

24

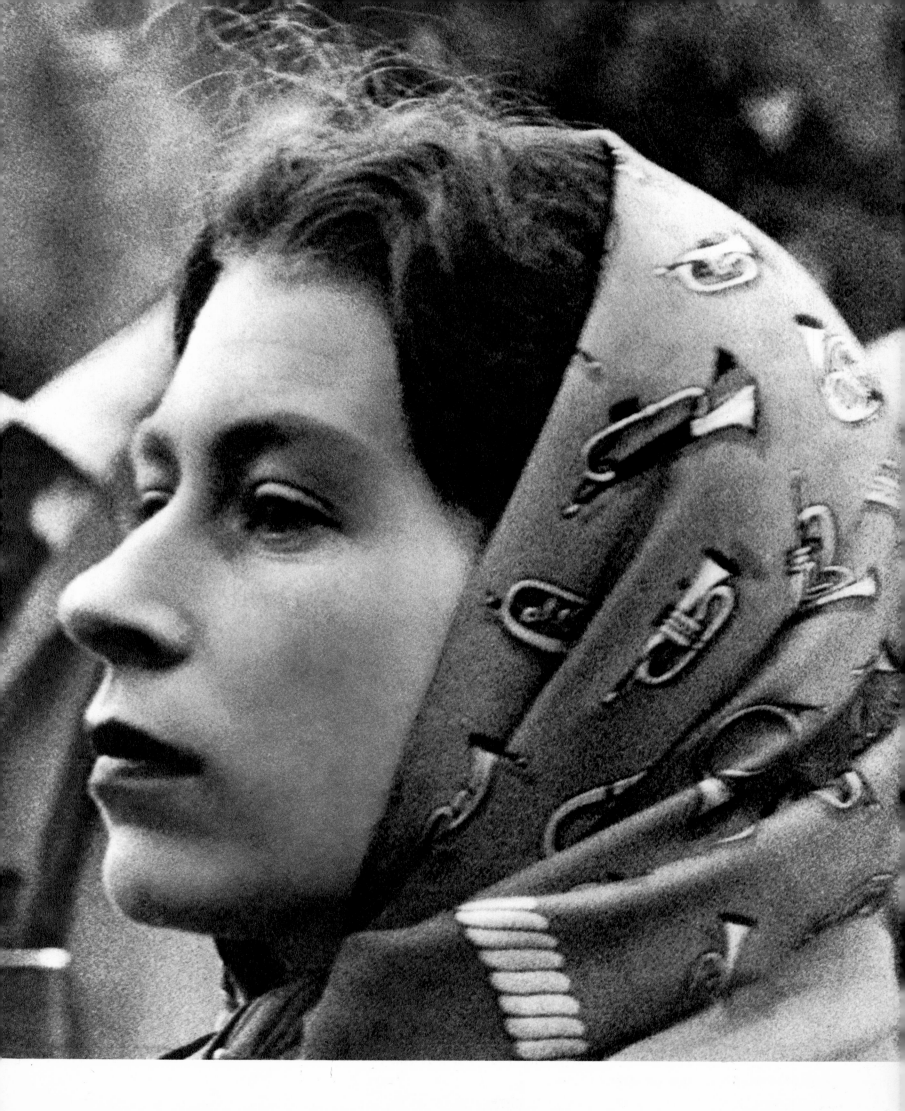

THOSE BEFORE HER

ANNO DNI · 1 5 4 4 ·

LADI MARI   DOVGHTER TO
THE MOST   VERTVOVS PRINCE
KINGE HENRI   THE EIGHT

THE AGE OF   XXVIII YERES

Mary I, 1553–1558

Elizabeth I, 1558–1603

Mary II, 1689–1694

Anne, 1702–1714

Victoria, 1837–1901

Elizabeth II

Queen Victoria in her wedding gown, 1840

King Edward VII and Queen Alexandra and their children ▶

Queen Alexandra in Coronation robes, 1902

Queen Mary in her wedding gown, 1893 ▶

King George V and Queen Mary.   Coronation 1911

Her Majesty Queen Mary

King George VI aged six, 1901

Queen Elizabeth, the Queen Mother, aged two, 1902

George VI and Queen Elizabeth as Duke and Duchess of York

Queen Elizabeth, the Queen Mother ▶

◀ Princess Elizabeth.   Glamis Castle, September, 1929

The Duchess of York and Princess Elizabeth, May, 1926

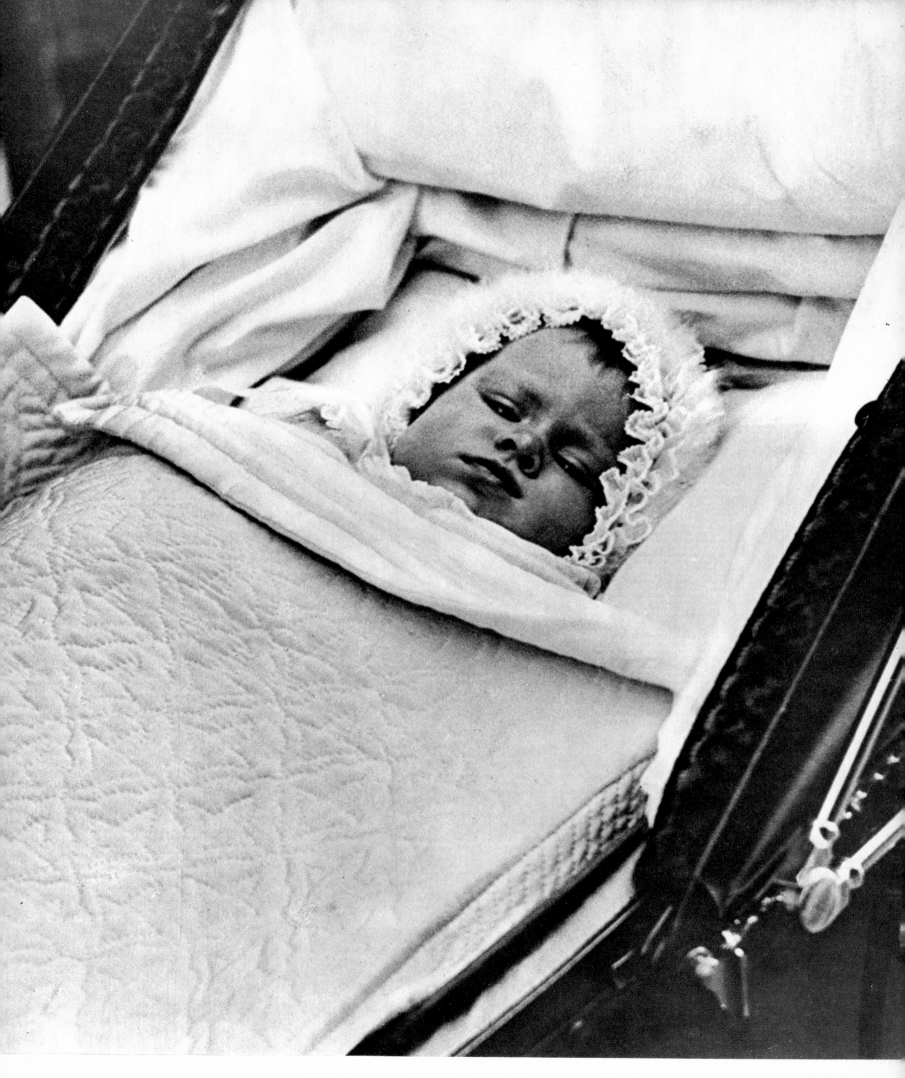

Princess Elizabeth

Princess Elizabeth and Princess Margaret, Olympia, 1935

The Princesses with the Duke and Duchess of York and
the Duke and Duchess of Kent.   St. Paul's Cathedral, 1935

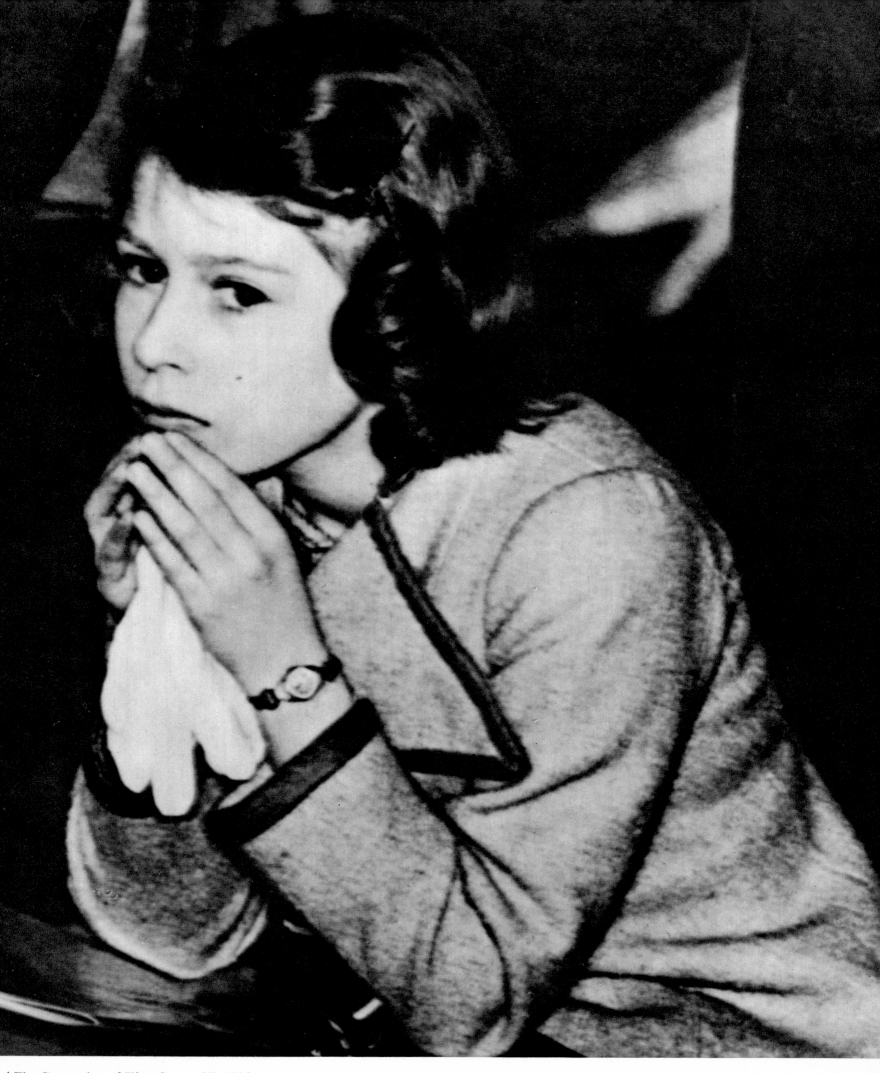

◀ The Coronation of King George VI, 1936   Princess Elizabeth

The Princesses.   Windsor Castle

The Princesses.   February, 1943

Princess Elizabeth on her fourteenth birthday, 1940

Prince Philip at school

◀ Queen Mary when Princess of Teck, aged twenty-three, 1890

Princess Elizabeth

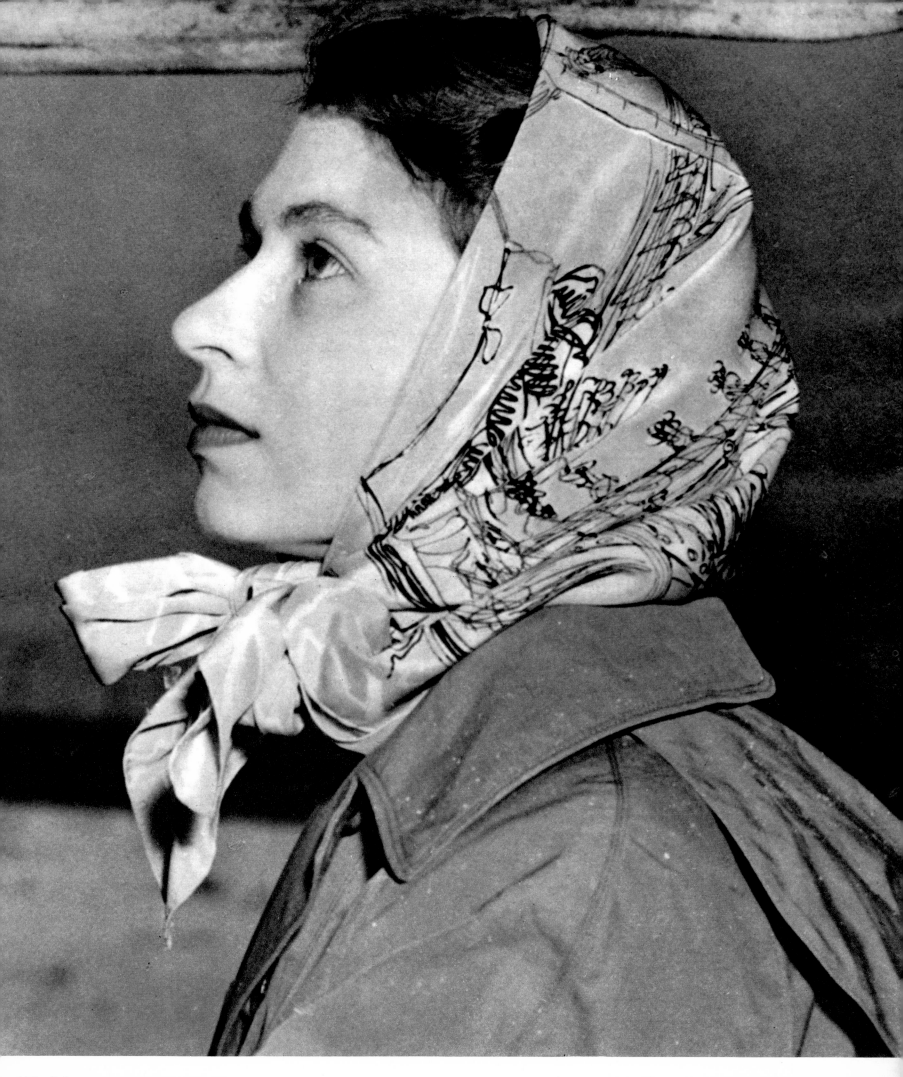

◄ The Princesses.　Royal Train, South Africa

Princess Elizabeth.　Royal Train, Alberta, Canada

The Engagement of Princess Elizabeth and Prince Philip.   Buckingham Palace, 1947

Prince Philip

The Bride.   Westminster Abbey, November 29th, 1947

The Bride and the Bridegroom

The wedding group.   Buckingham Palace

Queen Victoria and Prince Albert, 1855

Princess Elizabeth and Prince Philip, 1947

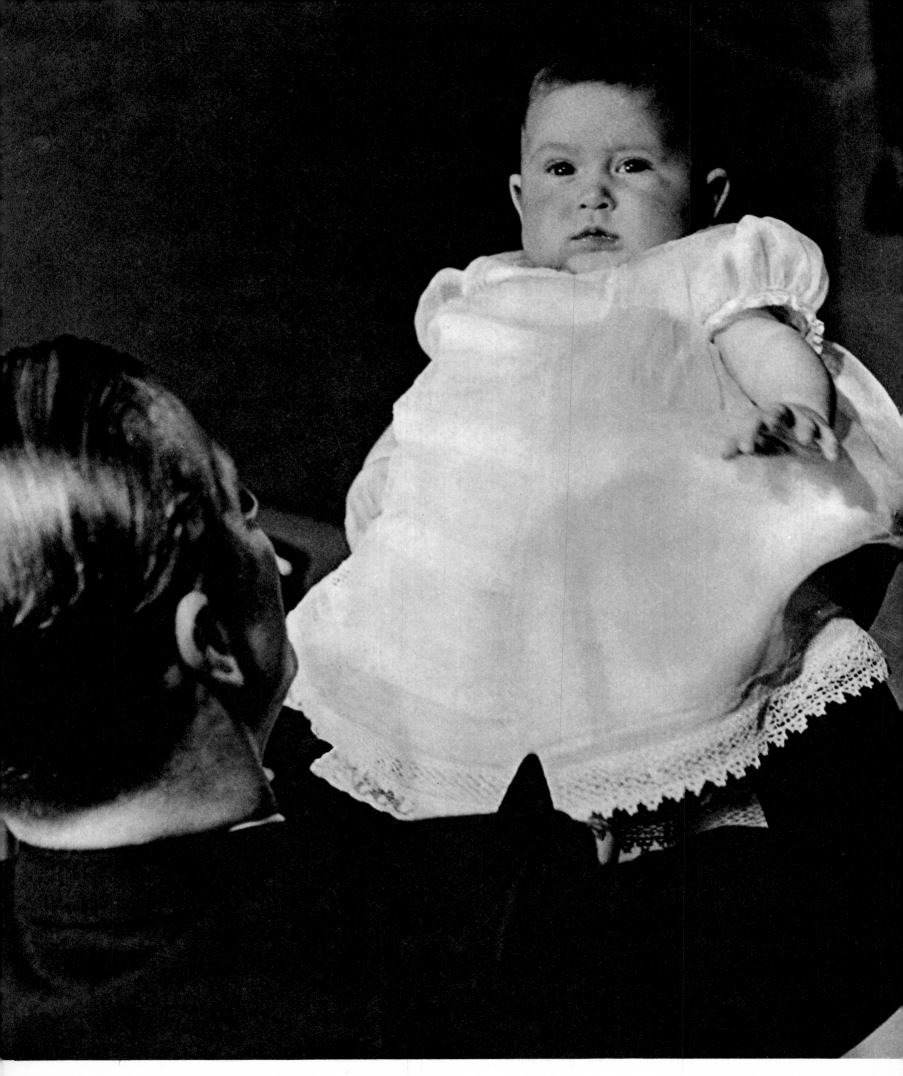

Prince Philip and Prince Charles, 1949

Princess Elizabeth with Princess Anne.   Clarence House

The garden, Clarence House

96

◄ King George VI with Prince Charles.   Buckingham Palace, 1951

The Farewell.   London Airport, January 31st, 1952

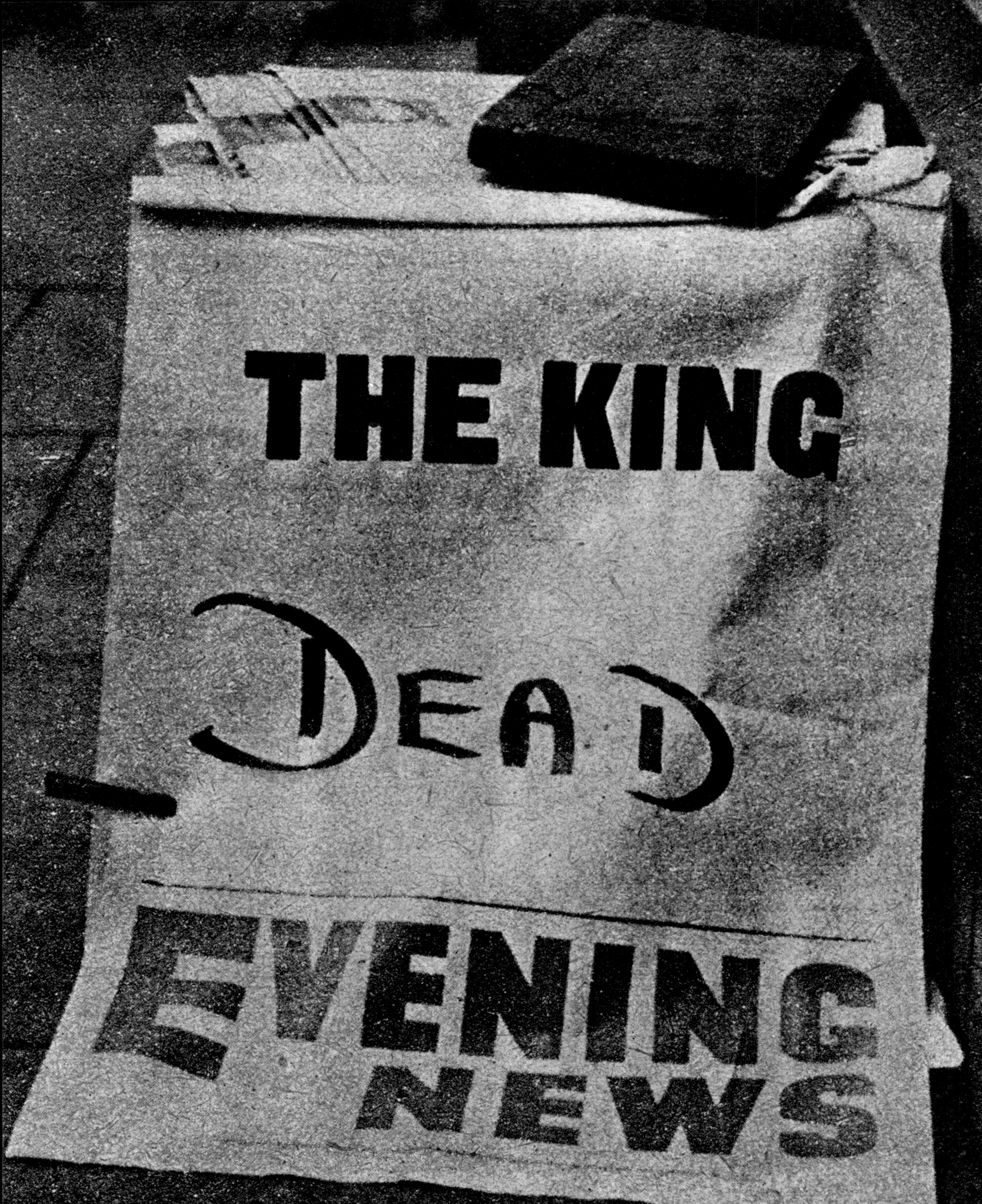
THE KING
DEAD
EVENING
NEWS

LONG LIVE THE QUEEN. Kenya, February, 1952

The return of Her Majesty the Queen.   London Airport, February, 1952

◀ Queen Elizabeth I

Queen Elizabeth II

The Queen leaves Buckingham Palace to open her first Parliament. November, 1952

The Drive to Parliamen

The Procession in Parliament

The Throne in the House of Lords ▶

Coronation Morning.   June 2nd, 1953

THE CROWNING

Detail of the Coronation Coach

◀ The Anointing

The Investing

Queen Victoria enthroned

Queen Elizabeth II enthroned

The Procession

136

142

Queen Elizabeth, the Queen Mother,
and Princess Margaret.
Coronation Day

144

Coronation Day. Fulham

Lillie Walk ▶

The Gallant Gloucesters

Royal Horse Artillery

◀ The Royal Yacht Britannia

PORTUGAL   The Golden Visit, 1957.   Belem Palace near Lisbon

Portuguese National Guard

The arrival of Her Majesty in the Portuguese State Barge

ITALY

Her Majesty the Queen at The Vatican

NIGERIA   Her Majesty greeted by King Adenji-Adele II.   Lagos, 1956

The presentation by Miss Ajibola Gibson-White.   Ijora

The presentation by Master Olubunmi Jibowu.   Lagos

Queen Elizabeth with King Adenji-Adele II

Chief Frank Griggs and King Mingi X of Membe

The Kaduna Durbar, Nigeria.
February, 1956

178

Camel boy.   Kano, Northern Nigeria

◀ Leper Colony, Oji River, February 9th, 1956

◄CEYLON Kandyian Dancers.   Matale, 1956.

The welcome by Sir Tikiri Banda Panabokke.   Kandy

AUSTRALIA   Palm Island aboriginals greet
Her Majesty.   Townsville, Queensland, 1956

Brisbane, Queensland

Hobart, Tasmania

Sydney.   The Queen and Prince Philip with the Prime Minister of Australia, The Rt. Hon. R. G. Menzies.   Farm Cove

NEW ZEALAND   Maoris at the Ngaruawahia Festival, 1956

PARIS 1957

VERSAILLES

VERSAILLES

HOLLAND Their Majesties Queen Elizabeth and Queen Juliana. Amsterdam, 1958

DENMARK · The arrival, Copenhagen

SWEDEN Stockholm, 1956

CANADA 1957

Calgary Stampede

The Opening of Parliament, Ottawa, October 18th, 1957

210

THE UNITED STATES OF AMERICA 1957
The Welcome by President Eisenhower.

The Queen addresses the Assembly of the United Nations.
New York, October 23rd, 1957 ▶

Washington, 1957

WELCOME QU

214

ELIZABETH II

HOME

The return to Buckingham Palace

Princess Anne and Prince Charles

Buckingham Palace

236

SCOTLAND ·

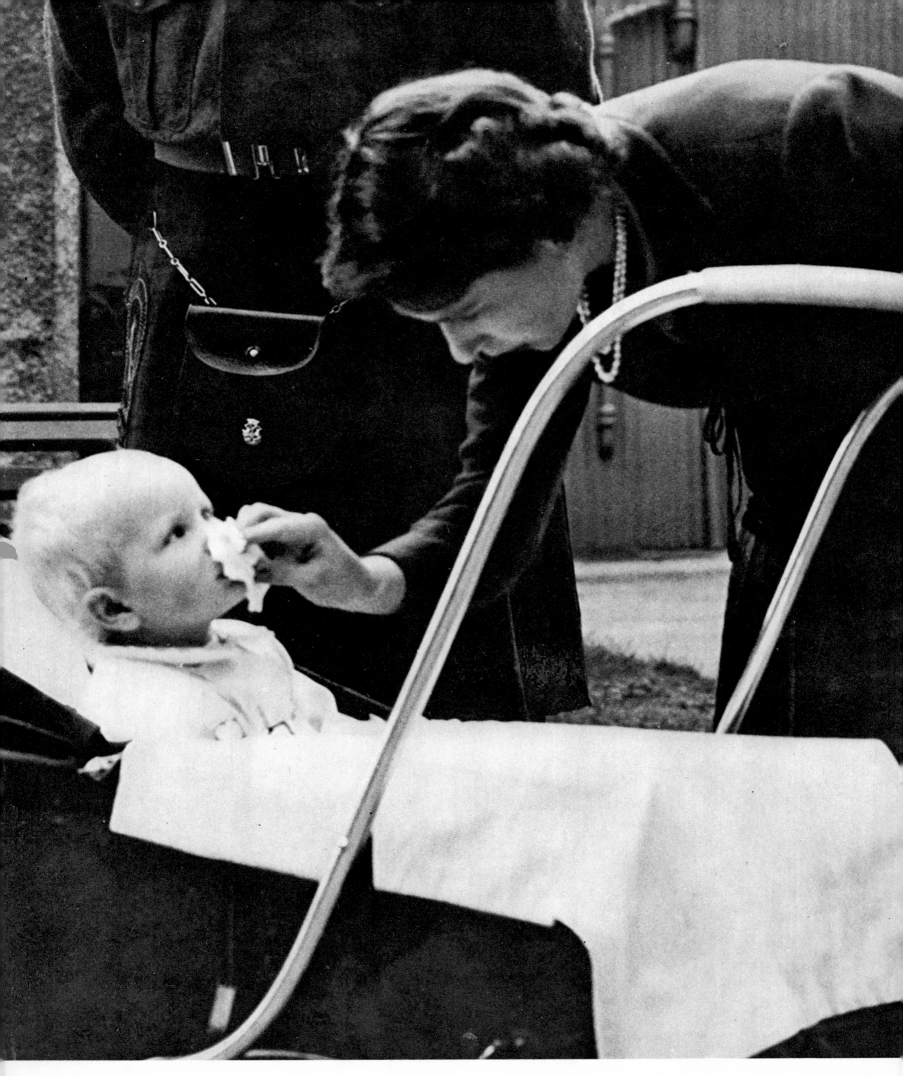

With Princess Anne

Braemar

Birkhall

6057

U-1-e   50%

WALES

SCOTLAND

Prince Philip as Colonel-in-Chief of the Cameron Highlanders

Buckingham Palace

The Throne Room, Buckingham Palace

NON SINE SOLE
IRIS

252

NOTES ON THE PICTURES

THE COVER These designs are reproductions of one of the allegorical panels by Cipriani on the State Coach, which has been used for Royal Occasions since it was built for George III.

THE END-PAPERS Facsimiles of all the recorded signatures of the Kings and Queens of England.

ACKNOWLEDGEMENTS

The editors wish to express their gratitude to the following for many of the photographs used in this book: The Photographic Department of the British Museum; The Hulton Picture Library; Associated Press Ltd.; The Kemsley Picture Service; The Harris Picture Agency; Keystone Press Agency; Fox Photos Ltd.; Dorothy Wilding; Studio Lisa; Graphic Photo Union; Black Star Ltd.; Camera Press Ltd.; Sport and General Ltd.; the Press Combine; The Harvill Press; the National Portrait Gallery; the United States Offices of Information; the Information Offices of Australia; the Information Offices of Canada; the Information Offices of New Zealand; the Vatican Press Offices; and the Press Attaché, the French Embassy.

The editors also wish to thank Mr. Cecil Beaton, Mr. Alec Murray, Mr. Tony Armstrong-Jones, Commander Michael Parker, Mr. Norman Parkinson, Mr. Rex de C. Nan Kivell, Mrs. Dorothy Searle, Mrs. Mona Parrish and the staff of the Hulton Picture Library, Mr. José Luis Pradera, Mr. Saville of the Kemsley Picture Service, Mr. August, of the Economic Photo Service, for their assistance and advice; and especially Mr. Frederick Fewings-Shorter for the typography in this book.

★

First published 1958 by

HUTCHINSON & CO. (Publishers) LTD

178–282 Great Portland Street, London, W.1

© Copyright HARRY TATLOCK MILLER
and LOUDON SAINTHILL 1958

Printed in monochrome Gravure and colour
Litho by JARROLD & SONS LTD, NORWICH